25.12.76.

Now you [barcode: D0364066] ng AND
the short of it ...

Alison & Martin.

Ronnie Corbett's small man's guide

RONNIE CORBETT'S SMALL MAN'S GUIDE

*edited
and compiled by
Spike Mullins
with illustrations by
Bill Tidy*

MICHAEL JOSEPH / M & J HOBBS

First published in Great Britain
by M. & J. Hobbs Ltd
25 Bridge Street, Walton-on-Thames, Surrey
and
Michael Joseph Ltd
52 Bedford Square, London WC1B 3EF
1976

ISBN 0 7181 1558 9

Typeset and printed in Great Britain by
Hollen Street Press Ltd at Slough
and bound by James Burn Ltd, Esher, Surrey

Designed by Lawrence Edwards

Contents

Foreword

May I just say thank you to the people behind the scenes. To JACK HOBBS who thought of the idea and to MICHAEL JOSEPH'S who fell for it.

To the nice people who sell books and the even nicer people who buy them.

And to the printers and typesetters without whose unstinting efforts half the authors in this country would have to go out to work.

Not forgetting PIERRE LAMONT of Saskatchewan, Canada, whose sturdy strokes laid low the forest giant from which the paper was made. Nice work Pierre, and be careful with that chopper cheri. There are not many of us good 'uns left.

And to BILL TIDY who did the drawings for this book. Anyone wishing to see more of his work should pay a visit to the Gents Toilet at Westbourne Park Station 8 to 5 weekdays, closed on Sundays and Bank Holidays.

And lastly I'd like to dedicate this volume to the Small Men who made old Britain great, men like Thingy and Whatsisname and others too numerous to mention.

And to SPIKE MULLINS without whom I don't know what I'd have done.

R.C.

The small man

1

and self-defence

> *And so I was fortunate that the first school I ever went to was a pretty soft school for pretty soft kids. Good heavens, at St. Pansy's Primary you could have a reign of terror with a balloon on a stick. We were paying protection money to the Brownies.*

Actually, in the first place, I suppose we should determine what we mean by a "Small Man". The whole thing is relative. If you live in England, where the national average is about five foot eight, and you are only five foot two—you are small. Whereas I was reading about a chap, smaller than myself, who went to live with a tribe of pygmies in the Congo, where he was known locally as Bwana M'Bongo M'Gongo, "He who walks with his head in the clouds". While that might be all very nice for some people, I personally don't feel inclined to trudge around the rain forests living on grubs and berries, just so I can look down on someone. Anyway my wife says, "It's too far from Sainsburys," so that's that.

I'm not sure it was M'Bongo M'Gongo – it might have been M'Gongo M'Bongo – but you get the general idea, don't you? Actually it doesn't really matter unless you're a pygmy, and if you happen to be a pygmy reading this book, well, Hullo Shorty!

Anyway that has cleared that point up, whatever it was.

So without further ado let's get right on with Chapter One, "The Small Man's Guide to Self-Defence". (I think I was right the first time, M'Bongo M'Gongo), but I digress.

Self-Defence. I suppose the obvious approach to the problem of survival for the Small Man is to avoid trouble in the first place, but unless you are going to join an enclosed order based on the teachings of St. Tyrone the Terrified and live in a cellar in Tibet, you might as well face the fact that eighty-seven point eight of all looping right-handers thrown in places of amusement – pubs – dance halls – other people's bedrooms etc – are thrown by *big* men and received by *small* men. And if you are going to go through life with beautiful thoughts about faith in human nature or memories of David and Goliath, you are going to spend more time in Casualty than some of the nurses.

Actually, it is an interesting fact that prior to World War Two, there existed a code of ethics that frowned upon the practice of big men hitting small men – especially *small men with glasses*. Then the Japanese declared war on us and suddenly half the world was full of *small men with glasses* running around, bent on doing a mischief to everybody. And it was during those dark days that society reconsidered the status of the smaller man and replaced the pat on the head, with a punch in the earhole.

Actually, there is more than one opinion regarding the merits of self-defence and the Small Man. There is one theory that the bigger the struggle you put up the bigger the whacking you are going to get. So the perfect ploy could be, as soon as the trouble starts, throw yourself down and pretend to be dead. This could possibly have the effect of frightening your assailant so much that, overcome with fear and remorse, he will immediately leave the premises and perhaps even the country. However, there's an old saying that murderers return to the scene of the crime, so just don't be sitting up at the bar giggling about it when he comes back or you might pay a surprise visit to the coroner after all.

There was a case recently of a certain S.M. who had learned Karate from a book, purchased in good faith from no less than W. H. Smith, or one of his Sons, and he happened to enter licenced premises where a multi-storey punchup was in

"— someone hit him in the face with the landlord's dog"

progress. Our friend stood quietly for a few moments on the fringe of the mêlée, a confident smile on his little features, considering whether to start his contribution to the action with a bit of fun, (chapters four and five) "How to bring about temporary paralysis by dislocation". Or to go straight in with lesson 28, "*For Advanced Students Only!*" "How to kill without causing unnecessary suffering". When someone hit him in the face with the landlord's dog, and as there had been no mention in the book about countering a blow with twenty pounds of cross-bred bullterrier, he panicked, went to pieces and started shouting, "Help! Police! My doze is mleeding!" and "The drinks are on me!"

Later his wife had to supply a photograph of what he used to look like before they could put him together again.

In any case the business of learning the Martial Arts from a book is very much over-rated.

Put yourself in the place of our friend, foolhardy little twit. You have survived the encounter with the aerial pooch, and gone in with lesson 28. Figs. 1, 2, 3 and 4, starting with Fig. 1. Grip your opponent's lapel firmly in the right hand, now, pivoting on your left foot – (is it possible your opponent hasn't got a lapel? Some suits don't have them these days! Hard luck, you've picked a snazzy dresser!) but by the time you have digested this information you are already into Fig. 2 and pivoting gracefully on the left foot, and unless your opponent is completely lost and overcome by the grace and beauty of it all, he is now in a position to give you a kick from behind that could leave you speechless for a fortnight with all your hair falling out.

Therefore it almost immediately becomes obvious that all those hours you spent in your little room giving a hard time to a couple of pillows inside an old raincoat, followed by the occasional Flying Lotus at Mummy while she is straining the greens, has got you precisely nowhere, and if you continue along this path you will eventually become a burden on the

The small man

National Health.

"But what," you may well ask, "about those schools where they teach Kung Fu and Judo and all that jazz?" Good question, and very nicely put, because therein lies the answer to our problem.

It was indeed a lucky day for me when in the spring of '75 I made the decision to become a student of the Kung Fu School of Martial Arts.

The Kung Fu School of Martial Arts is situated, as you may know, between the New Swedish Massage Parlour and the Novelty Sex Emporium, Dean Street, London W.1. When I entered the front office that morning I was greeted by a Chinese girl of such incredible loveliness – I think she was Chinese, but she could have been Japanese. They say you can tell the difference but I've never personally believed it – anyway she was so lovely that I had to go outside again and check the name over the doorway, because I thought for a moment that I had walked into the wrong place and was about to put myself down for some novelty sex or a massage by Bibi and Babs that might leave me even more vulnerable than I was already.

Anyway I said to her, "I'd like to – er – learn a bit of the old Judo." I've heard it said that you can't tell what the Chinese are thinking, because their faces are so impassive. But I could tell immediately that this one was thinking: "By the Sacred Buddah, we have a right one here."

"One cannot learn a *bit* of the old Judo," she replied, in a voice like the evening breeze rustling the cherry blossom.

I said, "Well I can't learn it all, dear, I'm a busy man, I've more important things to do. I just want to learn a couple of grips and armlocks and things to put a few of 'em in their place and stop them drinking my beer and fiddling the dart scores."

She looked very sad.

"Look, if I really like it and I get a bit more time I might go on to the more advanced bit, how to break their arms, etcetera."

I thought this might cheer her up a bit.

"Judo," she whispered, "is not for breaking the arms, but for strengthening the body and beautifying the mind." Her lovely fingers fluttered to indicate which was her body and which was her mind.

"Well," I said, "I think we can cut that bit by half, because while the body is obviously ready for some slight improvement I do happen to possess one of the most beautiful minds between here and the London Palladium. A puppy in a shop window brings an immediate lump to my throat and I have to be tranquillised every time I see Bette Davis in 'Dark Victory', so let's not worry about the mind, but concentrate the age-old skills and wisdom of the Orient on stopping me getting duffed up quite so frequently. Now let's say half a dozen lessons and see how we go from there. O.K?"

She bowed her exquisite little head to the Occidental ability to make up one's mind and pay the bill in 'readies', and wrote me a nicely headed Kung Fu appointment card. Then we relaxed a bit and had a little general conversation during which she told me she was married to a Karate instructor, which was the end of that.

But I always think that the few quid I spent that morning were the wisest I ever spent in my life.

I never actually got around to attending a lesson. I simply lost the appointment card several times in the various venues that I frequented and by the time somebody found it, and returned same, the whisper had gone round, "Don't take any liberties with him. He's a student of the Martial Arts."

The small man

2

and the law

> *When I was a baby I was found by*
> *a policeman on the doorstep.*
> *Not actually* on *the doorstep because*
> *the door opened outwards – I was found by*
> *a policeman halfway across the road.*

The small man

In this context the Law referred to is not the law in respect to legal jurisprudence because the Law as such is the same for everybody and makes no concessions whatever when dealing with the occasional lapses of the Small Man.

And the day is still far off when we shall hear a Judge pronounce, "Unfortunately, because of your lack of inches, the Law does not allow me to impose a fine or send you to prison, so go away and try not to get into any bad company." Which is a pity, and many of us Small Men will agree that such legislation is long overdue. No, the "LAW" we are dealing with here is the Law we refer to when we say to the wife, "Look at that car behind us, is it the Law? – the Old Bill – the Bogies – The Police stupid!"

Now the average person's relationship with the police (except in asking the time) falls roughly into two categories. He joins the police force or he gets arrested and, in a small minority of cases, both. But, first things first, and for the Small Man who feels that his true vocation is the enforcement of law and order the field is so limited it is hardly worth talking about. You will search for a long time before you see any police recruiting propaganda that invites applicants of good character, under twenty-five and *not less than five foot one*. In fact it would appear that the authorities are so obsessed by

"*The average S.M. would probably fail his medical to become even a copper's nark.*"

this question of height, that the average S.M. would probably fail his medical to become even a copper's nark. Which, according to what we see on TV, is a very important branch of the service, although unpensionable, with no boot allowance, and your only sports facilities, the chance of a short swim with a bag of cement.

Nevertheless, the possibility of becoming a sawn-off man-hunter should not be dismissed entirely because there must be other parts of the world where a five foot two inch copper would not be out of the question. "Ah," I can hear you say, "what about those aforementioned pygmies? I bet I could give a few of those a hard time and by so doing earn their affection and respect." But I regret to say that, once again, your hopes are dashed because there is no future for the mini "Old Bill" among the lads of the Congo Basin, simply because there is practically no crime in that area.

Thieving, for instance, is unknown, simply because nobody has got anything worth pinching and in any case where would you unload a bark loincloth or a hot bow and arrow?

And capital crime is so unusual among these people that it is hardly ever mentioned, except perhaps when creeping through the wet undergrowth on a cold morning, one might occasionally mutter, "This is murder!"

So until the rainforest mob get a few quid together and embrace civilisation, nobody is going to make a career out of locking them up, and they really weren't worth talking about in the first place.

Japan, on the other hand is a possible venue for the Small Man with a driving ambition to nick people, because here is a nation of Small People who logically must be brought to justice by small policemen. But while the Japanese crime rate is such that it is said the gendarmes do overtime adding up their overtime, the stumbling block for the average reader of this manual would naturally be the language problem. And I would be doing the reader less than justice if I were to minimise it, because however optimistic, I cannot see an applicant to the Imperial Japanese Police getting by without at least a working knowledge of Japanese.

And although the Japanese language when spoken sounds like an Irish navvy clearing his chest on a cold morning, I am told it is practically impossible to fake it – but to the Small Man who is really convinced that his rôle in life is to feel collars and give evidence in the dock, nothing is impossible, even learning Japanese; if they can do it, so can we.

So to encourage those among us who will not accept defeat, I have compiled below a list of the essential workaday phrases that you will need to start your career in the Tokyo Police Department. Once you have mastered these, the rest shouldn't be too difficult.

(1) Excuse me, sir, is that your rickshaw outside?
(2) If you bung me a yen, we'll forget all about it.
(3) Get your kimono and come with me.
(4) What are you carrying in that Saki?
(5) What are you doing against that pagoda?
(6) I know we all look alike but get in the lineup.
(7) Look out! He's got a geisha? (translator's note: some you win, some you lose.)
(8) Evening all.

3

The small man

and pets

> *When I was a little child my father*
> *bought me an earwig.*
> *Well, he never actually bought it.*
> *He got it off some people down the road*
> *who had more earwigs than they wanted.*

Now when it comes to the subject of pets I can say, without fear of contradiction, that I am a bit of an expert. That is one of the great things about writing a book; you can say what you like without fear of contradiction. I mean, if I were to make the above statement in the saloon bar or some other venue of free expression, somebody would be sure to say, "Excuse me, but I beg leave to question the validity of that statement," or "Shut up foureyes, you don't know what you're talking about." But as I was saying, in the whole of the western world, leaving out the Serbo Croatians and Grace Kelly (about whom so little is known), I am Jack the Lad when it comes to talking about man's relationship with his four feathered friends.

This comes about because I am a Small Man and the S.M. is indeed a special case when it comes to pets, because he, more than most, often needs a companion he can turn to for instant affection and no funny answers, and the obvious choice must be either one of God's creatures or a deaf and dumb nymphomaniac.

But let us take the first one first. And the marvellous thing about God's creatures is that they come in all sizes, so that you can choose between sharing your hearth with one of those dogs that go around dishing out free brandy to frozen monks, or you can hurry home to something that you have to sweep up before you know for certain it is still there. And the first consideration must surely be a financial one. In short, how are you fixed for the old pounds, kopeks, or drachmas, whichever you happen to be using? Because the St. Bernard could cost you about a hundred pounds down, and a pound a day for his meat. And this is of the utmost importance because it is no earthly good going home to a hungry St. Bernard without his rations.

An apology, however heartfelt, means nothing to a dog who has been brought up to expect perhaps half a reindeer or the occasional unfrocked friar. Whereas, to go to a somewhat ridiculous extreme, a common woodlouse will cost you nothing and a couple of matchsticks will last him a fortnight.

Although, let's be honest, if you really feel that you could strike up a meaningful relationship with a woodlouse, what you will need is plenty of fresh fruit and to get out more with people of your own age.

Actually when I was doing some research for this chapter, (and, for God's sake, books don't write themselves), when I was doing this research, I read of a Professor Hoffmeyer of Munich who in 1934 claimed that he had set up an unusual and somewhat revolutionary understanding with a common house-fly; and at the time everyone poo-pooed the idea. When Professor Hoffmeyer died he left his head to the local Medical College where they use it as a doorstop. But I digress.

Actually your choice of pet should be governed not only by what you can afford, or its value as a companion, but its interest as a conversation piece. Surely nothing could liven up your cocktail party like, "I say, has anyone seen old Spot the puffadder?" or, "Is that bloody gorilla still in the bathroom!?" Whereas, "Look everyone, my goldfish are swimming nicely tonight," will definitely get you labelled as a booby. So will, "Who wants to see a pregnant stick insect?" Although to be fair, they do say that goldfish have a great therapeutic value, inasmuch as if you are going to have a nervous breakdown and you do nothing except sit watching some goldfish swim round and round, it has a very soothing effect on the mind, although myself personally, I would just as soon have the nervous breakdown and get it over with. Because of all the wide range of creatures with which I have had a personal acquaintance, goldfish were easily the least interesting and our friendship, which lasted just short of three entirely uneventful days, was the least rewarding.

And I feel sure there were no regrets on either side, mine or theirs. I put them down the toilet and with a quick pull of the chain sent them off on a journey to some mighty ocean of their choice, to enjoy exotic sights and behavioural patterns that they would never experience swimming around on our sideboard, not since the au pair left anyway.

Of course no treatise on this subject would be complete without mentioning the ubiquitous budgerigar whose merry chatter makes him an ideal pet, especially for a person living alone.

There is a theory that a constant barrage of "There's a pretty boy!" could amount to a form of brain-washing and the bird's owner might find himself affected to the point when he had to glance in the mirror more often than is necessary and even spend his beer money on eyeshadow and a handbag.

But those are extreme cases and these birds do make wonderful companions when purchased from a reputable dealer. I have stressed this point because one cannot be too careful, and there have been instances when a surly and uncommunicative budgerigar has turned out to be a chaffinch with a respray.

Of course the list of creatures great and small which are willing to share man's hearth and board is endless, and each has its own particular drawbacks and advantages. For instance, you can strike a match on a tortoise which will accept it as a gesture of affection, whereas you will get a totally different reaction from a cat. However, there is no recorded instance of a tortoise catching a mouse, indeed it takes the average tortoise all his time to keep up with a lettuce.

However it has been proved over and over again, that man's best friend is a dog.

One has only to remember the epic adventures of Rin Tin Tin and Lassie to be reminded once and for all that there is just nothing like a dog.

Whoever heard of a budgie setting out to get help for his master left by some villains, awaiting a lingering death? A well-trained cat might consider the proposition, but a saucer of milk would change its mind and for an old fish head it would join the other side.

And a hamster would watch you being stamped into the carpet by intruders and it wouldn't be until the grub ran out a week later, that it would realise what had happened.

On the other hand, strangely enough, the porpoise, according to what I have seen on children's television, is not to be discounted among the short list of man's best friends.

The porpoise is apparently a very intelligent animal and faithful unto death, with an uncanny ability to grasp the fundamentals of a dodgy situation.

Let us suppose some baddies intend to spoil your lagoon blasting for the sunken treasure that was not theirs in the first place; your friendly porpoise will not only warn you of what is afoot, but will take an active part in dismantling the miscreants when the action starts and the chips, figuratively speaking, are down.

Mind you, because of his need for a subaqueous environment, the use of this splendid and sagacious animal to the average flat dweller is very limited, as is the probability of any intruders on the premises turning up in wet suits and plunging into the bath where you'd have to keep him.

At this point the discussion of the merits of this particular pet would seem to have become somewhat academic, with a touch of the ridiculous, and is best abandoned in favour of that

which we were concerned about in the first place – the old canine domesticus or common pooch.

Now when purchasing your man's best friend you must be very sensible and realistic. It is no good taking home something just because it is small, fluffy and lovable because if your residence does get turned over one night, Fifi will be the first in the sack with your transistor and the shield you won for your dahlias. On the other hand, you don't want an animal who looks as though he is just waiting to have another go at Red Riding Hood and who might make you spend half your evenings behind the sideboard with a tranquilliser gun.

When we do find the physically perfect animal, let us not forget that he has got to be fed and avoid being stuck with a canine gourmet who will wave us goodbye with his tail as we go up the steps of the poorhouse. Ideally, with all the facts in mind, we are looking for a friend for life who will live on garbage; a sort of faithful intelligent hyaena.

The degree of intelligence is very important because an over-intelligent animal can prove to be as big a nuisance as an idiot who has to be fitted with wheels because he can't remember how to walk.

In this context I recall the saga of a friend of mine who once owned a dog of super intelligence that could understand almost every word that was said to it and could perform tricks of incredible complexity. In fact his "roll over and play dead" was so realistic that when the animal eventually expired they had to get a second opinion before he could be buried. But secretly my friend was not all that sorry to see the last of his canine chum because the dog being so handsome and intelligent, two assets they didn't share, when they went for walks people would often stop and speak to the dog and forget to speak to him. My friend frequently returned home feeling very depressed and underprivileged, and it wasn't until the dog went that people started talking to him again. "Pity about the old dog," they used to say.

The small man

4

and the garden

> *There is an old chap who comes and*
> *amuses himself in our garden for*
> *a few hours every morning – and we've*
> *seen the police about him.*

Actually the first and obvious tip to the Small Gardener is not to grow any very tall flowers because not only will you not be able to appreciate their subtle coloration and get the full benefit of their delicate fragrance but you also might get lost.

And another little wrinkle even more invaluable that comes to mind is to go easy on the old insecticides, especially if you happen to be an E.S.M. (Extra Small Man) or Titch because what is lethal to a very large earwig might be a sufficient dose for you as well.

As a matter of fact, and since we are being frank with each other, it was such an experience that forced me to give up gardening some years ago almost as soon as I got started.

It was in the spring of '64 that I actually turned my first sod. Up to that time my total work in the garden had been to take the dividing fence down, in the hope that the chap next door would get confused and cultivate ours as well as his own. But his practised eye soon differentiated between our stinging nettles and his flower beds, and he made me put it up again.

It was actually my wife's idea that I take up gardening.

"Why don't you take up gardening?" she said.

There you are, I told you it was her idea.

"Why don't you take up gardening, it will make you fit."

I explained to her, as simply and patiently as I could, that

"*An important piece of advice to the small gardener is not to grow lots of tall flowers because you might get lost.*"

The small man

I was actually at the peak of the physical perfection required to do things that I needed to do, such as earning a few bob, drinking a few halves, an occasional game of golf Sunday mornings (if fine), and watching TV. If God intended me to win the Olympics or climb Everest, then I would answer the call when it came and prepare myself accordingly. Furthermore, what she was suggesting was in fact flouting the natural order of things, because there is no recorded instance of a man getting a hernia while reading a newspaper, or a nail in his foot, followed by tetanus, while watching his TV set.

But logic, however well assembled and beautifully conveyed, means nothing to a determined woman. And when it became obvious that sooner or later, like it or not, I was going to get out there and do some worm disturbing, I hit upon the idea of purchasing a book on the subject, which at least would show me the easy way. I might even find a publication that proves, once and for all, that gardening is bad for you.

But search as I may, I never did find an anti-gardening book. And it was not for the want of trying.

"Have you got 'The Evils of Gardening'?" I'd say brightly to the man on the bookstall hoping that he'd reply, "No, sir, but we've got 'Gardening Made Me a Cabbage' and 'The Cruel Soil' in paperback."

Eventually I settled for a tome entitled "Gardening Without Tears", because I figured that, as I am an emotional person and if I have to make the desert bloom, I don't want the neighbours to see me crying while I'm doing it. Strangely enough, after reading the book I became quite interested, so much so that I found myself buying gardening magazines and sending away for strange shiny cultivating instruments used, as illustrated, by lissom, laughing-eyed young ladies, after making their compost the easy way with "Agro".

Furthermore I'll be honest and admit that what with one thing and another, come the spring, I could hardly wait for the snow to melt to reveal the rich loamy soil that is my

heritage, etcetera. And by early summer that year I had
Dahlias, Geraniums, Michaelmas Daisies, those things with
spikey leaves, and Marigolds – you name it, I had it.

So one day I'm sitting out there reading a gardening
magazine with just an occasional glance round to see if anything has stopped growing, when I see this particular advertise-
ment. It says something like, "Mr. Charlie Earthbird of East
Lanarkshire has cleared his garden of every known pest with
only one application of 'KILLO' and has since won two cups
for his Dahlias." And there is a picture of Charlie surrounded
by his two cups, looking as happy as a man who has cleared his
garden of every known pest, *and* won two cups for his Dahlias.

It also says, "Don't delay – now's the time to spray." So
in no time at all I purchase my supply of "KILLO" and spray
everything in sight.

Two hours later I inspect the scene of the crime.

The caterpillars are still munching away like they've been
promised a bonus, and the earwigs are standing around in
small groups, apparently making plans for tonight. In short –
it's business as usual.

It's obvious that Charlie Earthbird up in Lanarkshire
is dealing with a weaker strain of pest than R. Corbett of
Wimbledon.

So taking a fresh tin of "KILLO" (one tin makes fifty
gallons), I dissolved it in a quart of water and hit them with it.
The effect was startling. The earwigs, caterpillars and green-fly
fell to the ground with hardly time to say "Goodbye" to
each other, quickly followed by all plants, a couple of sparrows
and next door's cat who happened to be passing. And the chap
who lives two gardens away, and has a bit of sinus trouble,
took to his bed and sent for the doctor.

And, personally, I nearly finished up in a jar on the
mantelpiece at the Institute of Forensic Medicine. It's been a
long road back, and I'm sorry, but if you want to know about
gardening you really are reading the wrong book.

The small man

5

and romance

> *My first romance was with a girl
> named Ethel Hardboard,
> she was thin but useful.
> We did our courting in a cemetery –
> me standing on a headstone and her
> with one foot in the grave.*

As soon as I had written the above title to this chapter the old memories came flooding back – the girls I used to know, Alicia Cadge, Madeleine le Fong, Cheryl Hitler, and Emily Slaggrader, who incidently changed her name to Arthur Slaggrader and turned out to be "one of the nicest fellers you ever met" and went on to do a trial for Q.P.R. The one thing that all these ladies had in common was that they were all ugly, some a good deal uglier than others. Actually, Madeleine le Fong had a slight lead on them all in this respect, and it was said that with no makeup, on a cold morning, she could stun a police dog.

At this juncture, you, gentle reader, are probably saying, "What care I about these camels you knocked about with, get on with the good advice while I'm still awake." And quite right too, and the reason I've mentioned these ladies, whose names, incidently, have not been changed (*because I know a very good lawyer who, if they start any sueing nonsense, will go round and break all their windows*), the reason I have mentioned them is to show that in my youth I fell into the same trap as nearly all S.M.s, in imagining that because of our stature, we don't qualify for the goodies that the others are getting. And of course this is nonsense. If Mickey Rooney married Ava Gardner so can we.

Was it not our own William Shakespeare who said, "Love

is blind"? He went on to prove his point by falling for Mistress Hathaway who, according to pictures taken at the time, was certainly no Miss World. In fact there are plenty of my acquaintances who wouldn't give her a drink if they were both locked in a brewery.

Anyway, let us presume that up to now you have had very little to do with the fair sex. Well, let's face it, if you were the Playboy of the Western World you wouldn't trouble to read this chapter at all. So you've been leading what to you has been a full and satisfying life going to work, making scale models of Winchester Cathedral out of matchsticks, and having an early night.

Now, presuming that you haven't got any cogs missing and all your genes are facing the right direction, you are sooner or later going to get the old urge. And it is no good taking notice of Mother when she says, "Don't worry Cholmondely, Miss Right will knock on the door one day," because the best Miss Rights are not going around knocking on doors, they are raving it up and getting valuable experience in blacked out discos before graduating to the Gin and Tonic Bar at the King's Head. Equally, you would be ill-advised to ask the girl next door, "If we can get up a team for a game of Doctors and Nurses in your tool shed, like in the old days?" because almost before you've finished the question, you'll be playing funny ink blots with a police psychiatrist. Nor is the Computer Dating Service recommended for us S.M.s because the computer will sort out someone of your own size and you'll go around looking like a pair of bookends, which can be very depressing.

No, what you have got to do is to give Winchester Cathedral a good kick up the nave and get out there where the action is. Bear in mind one or two golden rules such as:– A Small Man is more visible to the naked eye if he is smoking a big cigar and carrying a bundle of currency, because while some beautiful lady is probably just waiting to love you for yourself

The small man

alone, spending *money* is a great way of getting to know people. And you must have noticed that songs such as "I Who Have Nothing" and "Love is all I have to give" are normally sung by six foot two inch millionaires.

Wearing the right clothes is very important. After you've made the conquest you can put them over the back of the chair or please yourself, but you *should* be wearing them for the initial approach. So you can dispense with the blue pinstripe that was such a hit at Auntie Flo's inquest because if you walk into the company we are talking about wearing that suit, people are going to suspect that you might be a Mini Private Detective and most of them will utter small cries of alarm and disappear through the nearest exit.

No, if you are going to turn up at the King's Head smoking the Henri Winterman Corona and dragging the bundle of currency that you were saving for your holiday doing Brass Rubbings in Reykjavik, you've got to look scruffy not natty, because there is nothing more intriguing to the average female than small men, loaded with money, with the behind out of their jeans.

You will have noticed that we don't recommend the raving discos where the post graduates hang out, partly because you will need a very loud voice and a knowledge of the works of Frank Zappa to start a conversation, and also because the S.M. could easily get trampled underfoot and there is nothing more likely to cool the ardour than being trod on by a lot of strangers.

All females, even Traffic Wardens who manage to disguise it better than most, have an innate instinct to Mother somebody (SEE BUNNY GIRLS, PAGE 54) and while an average of one per cent take up nursing the sick, the others are dreaming of nurturing a neglected millionaire. And when the money runs out you can blame it on "Bad News from Hong Kong" or "The Angola Situation" or even "The Bloody Government".

Then, if you haven't made a permanent worthwhile relationship this time round, you can save up and do it again next year. And even if you never get to trot down the aisle with Ava Gardner, think of the tales you'll have to tell the gang down at the Lonely Heart's Club.

"*Nothing is more intriguing to the average woman than a small man with a big cigar, a large bankroll and the behind out of his trousers.*"

6

The small man

and history

> *Actually it was to one of my ancestors that King Harold at the Battle of Hastings spoke his very last words; he said, "Watch where thou art pointing that bow and arrow, thou wilt have someone's eye out in a minute."*

The small man

If one were to approach random members of the general public in the streets of London and say, "Excuse me but could you name some famous Small Men of British History?" seventy-eight per cent would name Napoleon Bonaparte, twelve per cent would call a policeman, two point four per cent prefer Max Bygraves and the remainder would be "don't knows" with a sprinkling of ignorant foreigners and blue film producers too busy to stop for a chat.

All of which proves that the contribution of us S.M.s to history has been almost totally ignored, and incidentally that London is going to the dogs.

Nearly all our National Heroes are biggies. And when you look at some of them a bit closer, they weren't all that fantastic after all.

For instance, what was so great about Alfred the Great? Here is a six foot hero who is said to have weighed in at about fourteen stone and is best known for hiding in people's kitchens. He would probably have never been heard of if, during one of his sabbaticals, he hadn't got into a punch up with one poor old lady over some cakes. Which hardly makes Alfred the Great a National Hero, does it? Or what about Robert the Bruce? Another man-sized legend in his own lifetime who, while the rest of the lads were battling away with whatever faction they were trying to make see reason at the time, was skulking in caves taking his mind off things by figuring out how a spider works. If a Small Man had done that everybody would say, "Well, what did you expect, cowardly little swine."

Did you ever hear of a cowardly big swine? Never!

To take another fascinating example. What made tall handsome Sir Francis Drake so famous?

"Sire, the Spanish Armada approacheth."

"Do they, forsooth? We'll murder 'em."

"A thousand ships of the line, Sire."

"I thought for a moment thou sayeth a thousand."

"That's the figure, Sire, give or take a galleon."

"Let's finish the game."

"But, thou has't finished the game, Sire."

"Let's make it two out of three, I feel lucky today."

Later –

"O.K. Let's make it the best out of twenty, I haven't hit my proper form yet."

"Sire, a storm has come up and destroyeth the Armada."

"Here finish the game for me, I'm off to get another knighthood."

You see, because it is only in recent times that it has become accepted that small is beautiful, most Small Men readily connived to avoid having their true height written into history.

I mean, would you have ever heard of Michel "Titch" Angelo, if I hadn't told you?

Did they ever tell you about Alexander the Short?

Did you know that if it had not been for Little Charlie Darwin, most of us intellectuals still wouldn't have known that we are descended from monkeys and not as was first thought from the milkman.

Did you know that Arthur Askey is more qualified to portray Mark Antony than Richard Burton? This is borne out

by Cleopatra's famous remark, "Hail Mark Antony, why are you standing in a hole?"

Of course, if Cleopatra had been born two thousand years later, she would have worn glasses and sized up the situation properly in the first place. Although if she had been born two thousand years later she wouldn't have met Mark Antony, so the situation would not have arisen in the first place.

And even in more recent times a lot of mystery surrounds the true height of many great men. Let us take a name at random, the late Professor Rutherford, Father of Nuclear Physics in this country. We rang up the Science Museum at South Kensington who should have known all about this great man.

"Hullo, is that the Science Museum, South Kensington?"

"Yes."

"Could you tell me, how tall was Professor Rutherford?"

Silence –

"You know, *the* Professor Rutherford, Father of British Nuclear Physics."

"Nuclear what?"

"Physics."

"Are you a spy?"

"Don't be silly, of course I'm not a spy."

"Now don't get stroppy with me Mister, we've got some of the finest brains in the world here and we'll come round and smash your face in."

"Look, all I want to ask is a simple question."

"We could answer any question you could ask, if we wanted to. D'you know how a steam engine works?"

"No."

"Well we do." CLICK.

See what I mean? It is possible that Rutherford was even smaller than me, but they just won't admit it.

7

The small man

and work

> *When I started in Showbizness,
> times were so hard that I used to lie
> in bed at night making plans to
> ambush Meals on Wheels.*

And let's face it, everybody be he large or small, has got to go to work. This is something that has been evolved by Mother Nature not only to make sure we don't starve to death, but also to get us out of the house for a few hours a day. This saves us from being murdered by the female of the species, which is especially adapted to drag rugs about while listening to Jimmy Young and discussing us with the Avon Lady, none of which can be done properly if we are still on the premises.

The trick is obviously to find something to do that will bring us the most return for the least effort. And clearly there must be jobs which, by virtue of his physical limitations and/or shortness, are not suitable for the average S.M. Statistics show us, for instance, that on average your five foot two male model will spend ninety-two point seven per cent of his working life looking for work, and the other seven point three per cent contemplating whether he is in the right job; a situation that can only lead to bickering and dissension when the woman in his life holds out her hand for the bread every Friday.

Let us therefore consider ways of turning an honest buck, pound or kopek, which are economically viable and won't get us into trouble with the police.

Personally I have found showbizness to be a very reasonable means to this end. The work as such is relatively undemanding, requiring only a certain flair for whatever you have decided to do, and then the nerve to get up there and do it.

And the possibilities of great rewards for the S.M. in this profession are almost limitless. Was it not Shakespeare who said, "There is no bizness like showbizness"? It might not have been, but he would have said it if he had thought of it, and whoever coined that deathless phrase (Irving Berlin, for instance) certainly knew what he was talking about, because there are a lot of people in showbizness who are getting more money than they can count, working less hours per night than the average burglar. After which, it's off to a nightclub for champagne and high jinks and a long lie-in in the morning.

It is however possible that this lifestyle does not immediately appeal to you. And if this is so, give it a few days and if you still feel the same have a quiet talk with your family doctor who will give you a bottle of Parrish's Food and get you certified.

But presuming you try showbizness and it doesn't work out, (and it has been known to happen, maybe the rabbit wouldn't come out of the hat, or the rest of the Young Generation couldn't keep in step with you, or your jokes were so clever the audience didn't start laughing until ten minutes later when Ken Dodd came on), anyway it's been a valuable experience and you can either jump off a bridge or look around for something else to do.

Perhaps you'd like to be a publican. Here is a way of making a living that is almost as good as showbizness because you are nearly always surrounded by people who are bent on having a good time. In fact the only thing missing is the applause, and sometimes that is absent in the theatre as well.

However the public house or trade booze dispensing is not always to be recommended to the *very* Small Man because you are not going to be able to do the affable Mine Host bit together with the jolly badinage if you are lower than the bar counter and all they ever see is the top of your head. Really, "Good evening, Sir and Madam!" is a bit off-putting to customers coming from a disembodied voice, especially if they've had a few across the road before they got to your place. And a courteous bow from the waist is a bit lost if you disappear while executing same because, for all they know, you could have fallen down the cellar.

The medical profession is of course wide open to the Small Man with a few 'A' Levels, giving as it does an opportunity to get around and meet interesting people with interesting diseases and often earning their undying gratitude – that is of course if they don't die. If they die you can't expect a lot of gratitude, especially if they only came in with acne or a headcold in the first place. But if you are a good practitioner this shouldn't happen, not often anyway.

It must be pointed out, however, that the possibilities of attaining great pinnacles of success in the medical world are indeed limited for the S.M. No one for instance ever did a heart transplant standing on a box, for the obvious reason that if you step off the end of the box at the wrong moment, a lot of essential bits and pieces could end up down there on the floor with you, and while the patient will probably never know what happened, the rest of the team are going to feel their efforts are being wasted and they might as well have stayed in bed.

On the other hand, to my way of thinking, being a solicitor always seems to be a bit of a pushover and it is an interesting fact that nobody ever heard of a poor solicitor. Starving actors are a common enough sight in most big cities in the world. Impoverished priests are not unusual, and the occasional fallen quantity surveyor has been sighted. But nobody ever opened his door and found a hungry solicitor huddled among the empty milk bottles for warmth. And if this were to

"*The very small man is at a disadvantage behind the counter of a public house because very often the customers can hear him but they can't see him.*"

The small man

happen you would be well advised to shut the door quickly because it is probably a trick to get you to sue somebody.

Actually going into the law, or as they refer to it among themselves, "Catching the Gravy Train", could be ideal for the Small Man with a streak of craftiness in his make-up, and most of us S.M.s are a bit crafty. We have to be to survive.

Actually the more you think about it, the more attractive the solicitor idea becomes. It's just as good as being a doctor because it has the same advantages inasmuch as the average person won't know what you are doing to him. He is afraid to ask, with the added bonus that none of your customers are going to call you at three o'clock in the morning and say things like, "Come quickly, I don't like the look of my wife, I think I'll divorce her." And just supposing that did occur, you soon put a stop to it by dragging him into court next day on a writ of Habeas Corpus, quoting the case of Jellyhead v. Ratthrasher 1581; immediately you have a restraint on his goods and chattels and a remand in custody until he is too old to remember what happened.

Of course, no list of opportunities for the S.M. would be complete without the most obvious, that of becoming a jockey. If you fancy the idea of finding yourself, half starved, jumping about on top of a large and unpleasant horse, a complete stranger to you, then you've got to be out of your mind. So much for jockeys.

The list is endless and if nothing I mentioned here appeals to you, you could drop in at your local Citizens' Advice Bureau. The possibility of doing better down there is a bit remote, except that you might happen to meet a millionaire's daughter doing charity work who is mad about Small Men, and then your troubles could be over.

The small man

and hobbies, pastimes

> *My wife said, "Whatever do you want
> a racehorse for? You've already
> got a dog." And I had to explain to
> her that with the best will in the
> world you can't expect a ten-year-old
> poodle to win the Grand National –
> it takes him all his time to put
> his leg up for the Oaks.*

The small man

Here once again we have an instance where the pursuits of the average S.M. need vary only a little from those of his friend the Large Man, or Oaf. And their interests, which may vary from pressing leaves in a book to collecting old Bunny Girls, may be entered into with the same enthusiasm and indeed the same possibilities of success. Although, to be mildly academic and at the risk of contradicting ourselves, in both the random subjects mentioned the Small Man does actually have a bit of an edge. You see, the large man with his hands resembling a bunch of bananas will most certainly spoil more of his leaves than will the small man with his nice, delicate little pinkies; he may in time become disheartened and turn away from leaf pressing to other pastimes such as decorative bricklaying, or mugging, for which he is better equipped.

And of course the Small Man has a certain advantage with Bunny Girls because of their super-mother instinct, inherent in all Bunny Girls. This is demonstrated by their cheerful willingness to serve and their fantastic mammery glands or "Charlies".

Incidentally, and it cannot be stressed too strongly, this particular hobby (collecting old Bunny Girls) naturally calls for an initial outlay of capital on a par with running your own space programme, so don't give up your lino cutting until you are quite sure this is what you want to do.

But let's take this thing out of the realms of fantasy and deal with the possible interests of the Small Man who hasn't got a yacht and thinks that leaf pressing is a bit poofy, which it is anyway, and I don't know how it came to be mentioned in the first place.

Angling. For the price of a rod and a bit of line and a few garden worms, (who it is said, enjoy nothing more than a day out by the river), you can have hours of harmless fun, hauling in such common and uncommon species as Bream, Perch, Pike and our old friend the Roach who, when cooked in a white wine and served with a bit of melted butter is said to taste not unlike the offcuts from a tyre factory.

There is, as far as I know, very little else to be said about fishing, although I do understand from a television programme I recently watched on the subject that some fish, even when hooked, are reluctant to come out of the water, and a two pound Perch will sometimes fight for more than an hour. So the obvious conclusion would be to avoid areas where such species are to be found because while you are battling away with brother Perch and his ilk, the other species, who are not so neurotic about the whole thing, will make their way to less noisy parts of the river and you could finish the day practically empty handed.

If you still wish to know more about fishing there are various books on the subject, the most famous of which is called *The Compleat Angler* by Isaak Walton. Although how a man who can't even spell "complete" has got the nerve to write a book, I can't understand.

Art can be a very rewarding hobby, providing as it does an opportunity to stare at nude ladies without getting into trouble for it, with the added bonus of being able to give up shaving and stop wearing socks. And if you are really small you can tell everybody that you are a relation of Toulouse Lautrec and they will be so pleased to meet you that you'll be able to turn up for classes with nothing but a biro and an empty cornflake packet.

And supposing you decide to advance further than simply enjoying the fringe benefits, it is surprising what you can get away with in the field of Art. If Picasso could get thousands of pounds for, say, a drawing of half a one-eyed lady contemplating a fish head, there is indeed hope for us all.

The trick is to be as confusing as possible. If Picasso had painted the above, if Picasso had painted it, he would probably call it something like "Murzerka" and all the art lovers would come along and say, "Well I never!" "Fancy that!" "Light and shade!" "Perspective!" and other appreciative artistic remarks, because for all they know, "Murzerka" is an old Ukranian cure for Athlete's Foot and not one of them is going to admit that they don't know.

So that when you get weaving with your box of paints and your painting of a lovely nude lady with a bunch of flowers turns out looking like the effect of atomic radiation on an unborn camel, don't chuck it away, call it something like "Premonition of Civil Disobedience" or "The Reincarnation of Bourne and Hollingsworth". As long as they haven't got the faintest idea what it's all about, you could be on a fortune.

Bird Watching. Here is a simple inexpensive hobby often thought to be of therapeutic value to the loner who feels the urge to wander lonely as a cloud whilst waiting for an answer from Marjorie Proops. And the Small Man is ideally suited for birdwatching because the smaller he is the less likely he is to be spotted as he creeps up to get a closer look. The average bird, which is not all that bright at the best of times, will often sit there thinking, "Christ, is that a man?" until our S.M. is close enough to study his plumage and even perhaps poke him with a stick. A sharp eye and a notebook and pencil are the basic equipment required, together with a packet of your favourite sandwiches and a bottle of lemonade or cold tea, or Redex and cough mixture, whatever you happen to be on at the time. And, pausing only to wave goodbye to whoever let you out, you can stride purposefully off into the countryside on a journey that might or might not lead to exciting discoveries, according to how easily excited you are.

And what better than to drop into a country pub after a tiring but rewarding day in the undergrowth. "I spotted Jenny Wren in Dingley Dell today," you say to the man sitting next to you. "Keep your voice down" he replies. "That's her husband selling the raffle tickets."

Boxing. There is sure to be a local boxing club in your district and if you want to go along and put your name down for a good hiding every Friday night, the more fool you.

Climbing. Here is a strenuous outdoor pastime with more than a hint of danger to life and limb and therefore best avoided. Nobody knows exactly what makes a man want to pit his strength and wits against a mountain. In fact when the first man to climb Everest was asked why he did it, he is said to have replied, "I don't know, but in future I think I'll stick to the bitter."

Darts. Membership of a local darts team offers the cheerful good companionship of a load of drunks, and the opportunity of travelling round challenging other teams and throwing up in different surroundings.

Excavating for old bones and things, or archaeological excavating to give it its proper title, is a hobby both interesting and at times rewarding. The tomb of the late Tutankhamen is said to be worth a million pounds and going up all the time.

Having said that I must point out that if you are seriously considering making your first million with a shovel, you would be better advised to forget archaeology and get yourself a job with McAlpines digging the new motorway.

In fact the discoveries of other amateur archaeologists are mostly of no more than interest value, such as fragments of Roman pottery which are very common because our Roman invaders had a pathological dislike of washing up, and after every meal would toss the whole twenty-one piece out of the window. Which of course is where we get the old Roman saying, "– – – – – the plates, let's get on with the orgy."

Freshly excavated building sites are a happy hunting ground for the archaeologist. But care must be taken to properly identify any finds before their removal, bearing in mind the experience of the enthusiast who thought he had discovered a statue amidst the rubble, only to find that he was carrying a Mr. Patrick Mahoney, employee of the Southern Electricity Board who had entered into a state of suspended animation for a period of overtime.

Exploring. Amateur exploring in this country is mostly confined to the discovery of underground caves. This is because everything above ground has long since been discovered and belongs to the Borough Council, The Abbey National Building Society (address on request) or the Duke of Westminster.

Underground exploration or pot-holing is normally carried out by teams of intrepid ladies and gentlemen who travel great distances under the ground to find new and undiscovered caves which I am told they sell to the Borough Council, The Abbey National Building Society, or the Duke of Westminster.

Golf. Golf is often regarded as an expensive hobby, and quite rightly so.

Jumping. And by this I presume I mean show jumping, although logically a Small Man's sport is something not to be undertaken lightly just because everybody said you were a natural on the donkeys in Benidorm last year. Remember that many of our leading show jumping personalities are often sober at the time of the event. And that nobody has ever got far in the show jumping world without a horse. And while you may play an occasional round of golf by scrounging a ball and, "Can I borrow your driver?", "Be a sport, Harvey," is not going to get you a mount in the 'Horse of the Year' Show.

So unless you are in a position to lay out the price of a horse, even a secondhand one, you might as well forget we even mentioned it. And if you do happen to possess that kind of money you shouldn't be reading a book, you ought to be out enjoying yourself.

Knitting. Knitting is a fairly simple undemanding pastime which is said to have a certain therapeutic value and as such is a rewarding method of unwinding after a hard day at the office or the shop or the rockpile or wherever you get to of a daytime. And once you've got the hang of it you'll soon be making a pullover or a scarf or a sock, or perhaps a pullover that looks like a scarf or sock. Can't you imagine how you will impress, say, the girl of your choice at the firm's dance?

"Mm, your hair smells nice. D'you like the cardigan?"

"Yes, it's very nice."

"Made it myself."

"You're joking."

"Four ounces of Angora three ply, number six needles, two plain one purl and did all the casting off myself."

"Wouldn't you sooner dance with my brother?"

So much for knitting.

Lino Cutting. For the price of some offcuts of linoleum purchased from your friendly local dealer, who I am sure will only charge you a few pounds because up to now he's been paying someone to take them away, you can, with the aid of a sharp knife, cut them into an interesting mosaic, pictures of crofters' cottages, pussycats and Concorde.

The art of lino cutting has declined in interest over the years until hardly anyone is interested at all. In fact many lino cutters have at times been so bored by the subject as to become absolutely paranoic, as is dramatically illustrated by the fate of such famous lino cutters as Mrs. Crippen, The Archduke Ferdinand at Sarajevo, Abraham Lincoln, and the crew of the Marie Celeste.

The small man

Rowing. From my limited experience I cannot recommend rowing as an enjoyable pastime. In fact one of the kindest things ever said to me by a fellow man was, "Come in number 27!"

Swimming. The sport of swimming has been enjoyed by mankind large and small since time immemorial, when early man noticed a frog swimming in a pond and thought to himself, "I wonder if I can do that?" And entering the water discovered that he couldn't and drowned.

After which, of course, swimming classes were formed to prevent the recurrence of such happenings. And to this day swimming classes may be found at most good municipal swimming baths where, for a small fee, the non-swimmer can join a class under instruction and become an object of interest to amphibious small boys. "Hey! Look at him!" they will shout and, "Can't you swim, Mister?" and, "Let's drown the poor old sod!"

Walking. Walking is generally regarded as a healthy outdoor pastime, requiring only the price of a pair of spiked shoes, a pair of football shorts, and an old vest which you have probably got already. And taken seriously, it could in time transport you from a morning toddle around the local rec' to the plaudits of your grateful country, and a Gold Medal at the Olympics. Although it has been said that competitive walking is not medically recommended for the S.M. because, his legs being that much shorter than other peoples, he really has got to twinkle to keep up, thereby throwing an undue strain on the old Gubbins Muscles which could come undone, and they would have to take you home in a sack.

Winemaking. Winemaking is a very satisfying hobby that has progressed in popularity in recent years, and many a hitherto neglected garden shed, or converted coal cellar now echoes to the happy shouts and laughter of a group of amateur wine makers, "Fill 'em up!" they shout, "I love you!" and, "Who am I?"

This resurgence in the popularity of the manufacture of amateur happy juice is due largely to the efforts of the chainstore chemists who, by cunning expertise, have simplified the process of manufacture and fermentation until a Burgundy can become vintage while you are stirring it in the bucket; and a Chablis that was laid down last week will prove its strength and character by dissolving the end off a spoon.

So no more the tedious trudging up and down on a bathful of grapes, and gone is the old nightmare of the wine maker where the plug comes out and he is left with nothing to show but half a bath of mush and blue legs.

For the less discerning palate there is of course beer making, and for the outlay of a few shillings the beer drinker, or guzzler, can blow his kite out with such brews as Newcastle Brown, Leamington Light, and Berkhampstead Bitter, all of which will lead in time to such excesses as cribbage, dominoes, and persistently seeing a man about a dog. But as my old Sunday School teacher used to say, "Whatever turns you on kid."

Yoga. According to my researches on this subject, which amounted to a quick free read of a book in W. H. Smiths, Yoga can do almost anything for you including mending your marriage to postponing that nervous breakdown that you've been looking forward to.

Although, to be honest about the marriage bit, I would have thought that if your wife can appear in court with a picture of you sitting half naked on the living room carpet with your legs round your neck, the Judge would give her an immediate divorce backdated to 1946.

"Learn to breathe," it says. Well up to now I had always been of the impression that if you didn't get the hang of the breathing drill as soon as you entered this Vale of Tears you went straight from the womb to the tomb and were never heard of again. And in any case if all of us carried out the exercise on page 15 fig. 4. 5. & 6., we would be using so much

oxygen that within no time at all wouldn't be able to get our hands on a mouthful of the stuff for love nor money. The only survivors, among the world's two thousand million population, would be the board of directors of the British Oxygen Company where they turn out those iron bottles full of it. And when you think about it – the rebirth of the human race from the loins of the Board of Directors of British Oxygen, two secretaries and a tea lady, is a thought that qualifies for a chapter on its own, and is indeed an idea that, given the right cast and some good music, might run for years on the London stage and make someone a fortune.

I digress, as ever, and as I cannot possible attempt to cover every aspect of the subject in the space available herein, I suggest that anyone who wishes to know the rest of it, should spend an hour or so in their local bookshop reading, "Yoga for Beginners".

This is a fairly wordy little tome so the reader is best advised to take two bites at it, such as reading to about halfway, Chapter 14, "Pelvic Enlightenment". Then take a mooch round the Record Department before attempting the rest, because some of those bookshop people can get very shirty if they tumble that you are prying and not buying.

Zurdling. Zurdling is a pastime said to have been very popular during the early Middle Ages in certain parts of Somerset where they no longer play it and indeed deny practically all knowledge of it, claiming it was brought over by the Normans, who took it home with them when they left, somewhere between 1128 and twelve o'clock.

9

The small man

and home decorating

Our old house was hardly worth decorating. Actually I had an idea that it was down for demolition when I came home one night and found two men marking out a motorway on the living room carpet.

c

Now, to the Small Man, home decorating offers very little more in the way of a challenge than it does to the normal size, except that the Small Man has to stand on a bigger chair to reach the hard bits. After that, it is very much the same for both, and during the decorating of, say, a bedroom, each will run the normal gamut of emotions, starting with enthusiasm, into annoyance and then despair and self pity. (The "Why me?" syndrome, Freud called it.)

Incidentally, the suicide rate among the home decorators is estimated to be almost double that of amateur car mechanics. But the exact figures are hard to come by because nobody can say for certain when the subject puts his finger in the light socket, whether it was a moment of thoughtlessness or whether it was directly related to the brush falling into the paint, and splashing the new wallpaper. So what actually are the alternatives to home decorating? The first, easiest and most economical alternative is not to decorate. This attitude, although frowned upon by the houseprouds, has among its devotees, many "exdoityourselfdecorators" who turned away from the practice after falling off a sideboard or throwing a bucket of paste over the wife. And they are now living happy normal lives by simply using low power light bulbs when they have visitors.

The other choice is, of course, to contact your local builder and decorator who will send one of his best men along within weeks of being assured that the room in question is empty of furniture.

The important thing to remember with the painter and decorator is to establish a good relationship from the start, because a good painter and decorator can be a friend for life or, in the case of a small room, perhaps for half that time.

A bond of mutual respect must be established, bearing in mind that he has been in the game for forty-seven years and he knew the area when it was a water meadow. He also knew the man who built your house and who was never brought to justice for it.

A cardinal rule is never to interfere with anything. He himself knows exactly which of his dust sheets are going to be spread over the floor and which of them he is going to use for building his nest in the corner of the room.

Other little points are, never, when serving his tea every hour, *never* push the door open without knocking because he might be mounting his pair of steps on the other side and a nudge, however gentle, will be construed as a deliberate attempt on his life, and as he is bound to be large, any rapport you have built up may well be broken and will take a long time and perhaps two ounces of Golden Virginia to build up again. Also, never attempt to socialise, except maybe at Christmas and on the children's birthdays, when they should be allowed to take a piece of cake into Uncle Painter.

So there you have the three alternatives.

1) Do it yourself, which to some has proved a valuable and testing experience and to others a short trip through the Valley of the Shadow terminating in a visit to the Booby Hatch or Laughing Academy.

2) Never decorate, and become in time a suburban troglodyte or cave-dweller, a source of concern to the neighbours and perhaps one day a guest on Nationwide.

3) Invite a stranger into your home who in due course will probably teach your children to read "Racing Form" when he is not discussing your personal shortcomings with your wife.

Now which is it going to be?

You've decided to do it yourself? A wise decision without which this whole chapter would have been a bit pointless. And if you stick closely to the following instructions and carry them out quickly and cleanly, you may emerge practically unscathed and the better man for it. So here we go and the best of British.

First put everything inside the room outside the room. Not too far outside the room or some of it may overlap into the street and fall prey to a roving junk man. Now the room is nice and empty. The room looks so much bigger, that there is a tendency at this stage to consider getting rid of some of the family and buying a snooker table, but the laws of the land being what they are, you are wasting your time standing there thinking about it, and you will be best advised to get on with the job before you make yourself depressed.

And a tip very well worthwhile remembering for the Small Man with a high ceiling who has to elevate the chair by placing household objects under the legs, is that there is nothing to beat a set of good old *Encyclopedia Brittanica* for this purpose, four starred for safety by the Society for Prevention of Accidents.

Whereas, on the other hand, old *Punch* annuals, *Ruffs' Guide to the Turf* and *Burke's Peerage* are in this context often referred to as the Widow Makers.

First the ceiling. What we need now is a bucket of whitewash, a big brush and a chair to stand on. If you haven't got a chair, borrow one from next door, or do the best you can.

Before commencing the ceiling it is a good idea to tie a piece of string tightly round your waist. This prevents the whitewash that runs down your sleeve going right down into

"*A good idea before commencing the ceiling is to tie a piece of string around your waist. This prevents the whitewash from running down your arm and into your boots.*"

your boots. There is actually nothing more depressing than sloshing about all day with your boots full of whitewash. Right, that's the ceiling done, good heavens it looks better already, doesn't it?

Now you can rush down to your local vendors to purchase a gallon of emulsion for the walls, or you can get it the same way as you got the whitewash – it doesn't matter as long as you don't get caught.

Next the walls. Take your brush in one hand and the tin of emulsion in the other and stand on your chair facing the wall. Not *too* close or you won't be able to see enough of the wall to make it worthwhile, and not too far away, otherwise you will be able to see *all* the wall, but you won't be able to reach it. The brush action for the walls is the same as for the ceiling, only sideways.

Try not to get too much on the door or you might not be able to find your way out again.

For the paintwork, you'll need a tin of paint and a little brush. Open the tin by means of the lid which should be on the top – if the lid is on the bottom you've got it upside down. Open the tin of paint, I hope it's your favourite colour, dip the brush carefully in the paint and rub it all over the wood-work.

If the result of all this is a disastrous eye-sore, you must do what you should have done in the first place –

either

a) move house

or

b) buy the wife a new coat and make *her* do it ! – after all she's bigger than you, stronger than you, and can reach all the difficult bits without standing on anything.

10

The small man

and motoring

*I had quite a few drinks at the
studio party last night, and when
I left there I went up the road,
twice round the roundabout,
hit the back of a 47 bus and finished
up in a chemist's doorway on the other
side of the road. I remember thinking,
Thank God I didn't bring the car!*

The small man

Here is another of those situations where the Small Man's problems are pretty well identical with those of the large man. Petrol costs the same regardless of the height or weight of the purchaser.

And if you are going to tell the magistrate that you didn't put any money in the parking meter because you couldn't reach the slot, you might as well plead insanity and a deprived childhood; you'll have to pay just the same in the end. And, "Hullo, sailor, can I take it home and blow in it?" will get the same reaction from the policeman whoever asks the question, and you will ultimately end up in the same kind of cell, be you large or small.

However, be that as it may (a stupid phrase when you think about it; I just hope I don't have to use it very often, but that is neither here nor there); however, let us presume that you have never driven a motorcar. You are, as they say in religious circles, in a "state of grace" at least as far as motoring is concerned. Whatever else you get up to is no concern of mine, although if you really want to unburden yourself I promise I won't laugh.

The first question you must ask youself is, "Why do I want to learn to drive a motorcar?" To which you will probably reply, "Because I am not having many good times waiting at bus stops." – and for heaven's sake whose fault is that? The next rainy night you're in the bus queue why not start things going? "I spy with my little eye something beginning with B." This is sure to bring a response from at least one of them. "I am the husband of my sister's wife, who am I?" never fails to start an interesting exchange of views. Or what about the old conundrum where the farmer takes six geese and a fox over the river without making at least one journey? That is always a winner for getting people together. In fact it was while testing the practical application of it, that six total strangers were run over together while rowing across the Edgware Road on a dark Thursday night in January 1957.

You still want to be a motorist? Then you have got to learn to drive, and don't let anyone kid you that you are going to enjoy the process, because it is during the first few lessons that the average person takes on most of the symptoms found in an advanced case of the dreaded Hopkinson's Disease, staring eyes, dry throat, stomach cramp, paralysis of the lower limbs, and a morbid preoccupation with death. However the condition will eventually pass, unless you have contracted Hopkinson's, in which case you must make your own arrangements, and good luck.

So, all things being equal, sooner or later you are going to take your driving test, this is practically unavoidable. Practically, because I did get a card through the door a long time ago from The Taj Mahal School of Motoring and Curry Parlour, Bombay, Dulalai and Hackney Wick. Mahouts to the Gentry, Weddings and Deliveries, objects no distance. This week's special offer, "Buy your licence from us and learn to drive in your own time." And I expect I could find it for you if you really want it. Nobody can actually tell you how best to pass the test. I suppose the most likely performance would be to conduct yourself as though you were driving the getaway car for a firm of illicit funeral directors, if you know what I mean.

The small man

Some people take a little drink before the test to steady the nerves, which is all right if you don't overdo it, because a remark like, "Come on bleedin' misery, singup!" will in most cases prejudice the examiner and you will have to be really spot on with your Highway Code to get him on your side again.

In any case, you are almost certain to fail on your first few attempts. *You* will know that your driving was immaculate but he will fail you on stupid things like, "Misuse of a shop doorway during your three point turn," or "What to do on a hump-backed bridge?" And just when you've got to the stage when you have begun to suspect the whole thing is an International Communist Conspiracy to drive you round the twist, the Examiner, obviously under pressure from the Council for Civil Liberties, decides to pass you as competent. It happens that way, believe me and have faith. And now for the really big moment, you are actually going to buy your very own motorcar. This is an occasion that most of us never forget, and one far off day, when you are sitting dreaming in the chimney-stoop, you'll say to your great grandson, "I remember when I paid four hundred pounds for a secondhand Vauxhall Victor."

And he'll climb upon your knee and say, "Shut up, you bloody old fool."

Nevertheless, this *is* your big moment, and if you'll take my advice you'll savour it alone, sans wife, sans friends, sans advisers.

"But," I hear you say, "I have never bought a motorcar before, won't I get screwed, conned, or taken to the cleaners?" Yes, of course you will, but the presence of a few amateur experts means nothing more than an enjoyable challenge to the car salesman and he will merely set his sights on lumbering you with a bigger load of old junk than he would otherwise have done. However, please dear reader, do not allow me to leave you with the impression that all car dealers are without honour. I recall the experience of a friend of mine who left

"*When he traded his car, he accidentally left his glass eye in the glove compartment.*"

his spare false eye in the glove compartment of a car he traded in, and within twenty-four hours the eye was returned to him, in mint condition, and no questions asked.

Now what kind of motorcar have you been dreaming about? The ideal car has actually not yet been manufactured, although it would be so simple in design having only one seat, that for the driver, so as to minimise passenger interference, and would be built by Krupps of Essen, whose Mark 111 Tiger Tank was so highly regarded by friend and foe alike during World War Two. So alas, until that happy day, you will have to settle, like the rest of us, for a standard family saloon that can be almost written off with a well-aimed blow from a bunch of flowers.

So one day you wander with ill-feigned nonchalance into your first car showrooms. You pause to drink in the aroma of acres of polished plastic and bathe in the reflection of tons of glittering chrome – and you run a tentative finger over the bonnet of the nearest bargain.

"She's nice little job, isn't she?" The salesman has materialised at your side. Car salesmen don't enter or approach, they materialise. "I said, she's a nice little job."

"Yes."

"Are you a Jensen man, sir?"

"Er, no, not exactly."

"I thought perhaps you were, the way you put your hand on the car, sir."

"Did you? No, as a matter of fact, I'll be honest, I've never bought a car before. This'll be my first."

"My cup runneth over."

"What was that?"

"I beg your pardon, sir, a small quotation from the scriptures. I had just finished my private devotions in the back there as you entered, a slip of the tongue as you might say. I apologise."

"That's all right, not a churchman myself but – nice to meet someone – you know what I mean?"

"Exactly, sir, and if my rosary gives you any offence then I'll put it back in the office, just tell me."

"Not at all."

"Thank you. Now this little beauty that has obviously caught your eye has a very interesting story attached to it."

"You don't say."

"It belonged to the only son of a titled lady who bought it as a birthday present for him before he ran off and married a chorus girl. Naturally she disowned him and the car stood in her garage with only twenty-four thousand on the clock for the next fifteen years. And she sent for me recently. 'Mr. Mendlebaum,' she said, 'I'm getting too old to polish Jeremy's car every morning, so I want you to sell it for me, and I don't care how much you get for it as long as it goes to a good home.' Isn't that a lovely story sir?"

"It certainly is."

"So I said to her, 'Your Ladyship, I'm going to forget I'm a business man and I'm going to knock this car out for a ridiculous price to someone who will love it as you have done, 'God bless you, Mr. Mendlebaum,' she said, 'now I can die happy.' "

"And how much is it?"

"To you, sir, fifteen hundred, no, we'll make that twelve, that's two fifty deposit and the rest over two years and you can sign the papers now and drive it away before I come to my senses."

So now you're a motorist with your own car that will give you hours of pleasure during the next few years. Soon you'll be able to take your place among the men when they are talking man's talk in the saloon bar. You'll be able to say things like, "When he said forty to the gallon I thought he was talking about petrol, not oil." – and: "Lucky I was on the inside lane, me two rear tyres blew out and a con rod came right through the bonnet." – and: "It was just after I got the bill for the new gearbox that I had my nervous breakdown."

The small man

At least the old gang at the bus stop used to say things like, "Good morning," and, "How's the wife?" And not, "What the hell do you think you're doing?" and, "Pull over, we want to have a look at your tyres."

11

The small man

and doctors

I haven't got much faith in the Studio Doctor because I knew him before he worked his way up, when he was a patient in Emergency Ward Ten. *An* outpatient – *he wasn't even worth a bed and a dressing gown.*

Now before you get yourself over-excited, dear reader, I must be honest and admit this is not going to be a brilliant exposé of the medical profession. So if you are looking for, "Doctor had me on the National Health," says model, "I only did it for the Cherry Linctus," or, "G.P. posed as window cleaner," sobs young housewife – then you are indeed reading the wrong book, because this is actually more in the nature of a copout, with the object of getting myself back in the good books of the healing profession. You see, every comedian big or small, tells "doctor jokes", and everyone who tells doctor jokes knows that he is pushing his luck a little more with each one, because somewhere at some time he is going to find himself at the mercy of a medic who, to use medical terminology, has had a *gutful* of being made fun of and is just waiting to get his own back.

I mean, it is possible that I will go on television tomorrow night and do a doctor routine including such gems as –

"If you go to Harley Street, they can tell what's wrong with you simply by feeling your wallet."

Followed by –

I said, "Where shall I put my clothes, doctor?"

He said, "Put them over there on top of mine."

And –

"Tell me, doctor, after the operation, will I be able to play the violin?"

"Yes, of course you will."

"That's funny, I couldn't play it before."

Straight into –

"Doctor, I had a hell of a job swallowing that big white pill you gave me."

"That wasn't a big pill, you fool. You've swallowed the box, the pills were inside."

"Oh dear, will it harm me?"

"Not unless the lid comes off."

Finishing with –

"If you put yourself in my hands you'll live to be ninety."

"But I am ninety."

"There, what did I tell you?"

Or –

"Doctor, I keep getting this terrible pain all down one side."

"That's funny, so do I. I wonder what it is."

So the whole nation falls about laughing, complete strangers, helpless with mirth, holding on to one another outside the telly-shop window; in some cases so carried away that some are arrested and others have to get married. In short everyone is having a great time, except one man, my own doctor, who is sitting there muttering, "O.K. shorty, the next time you come to me with a boil up your beak, I'll make your eyes water for a fortnight, you see if I don't!" This is not by any means beyond the bounds of possibility. If he wants to be *really* evil, the next time he gives me a letter to take to the specialist, what is to stop him writing –

Dear Aubrey,

　　　　　The bearer, Mr. Corbett, has applied for the post of Comedy Eunuch to the Sheik of Araby. Please make the necessary alterations and charge him double.

Squash Friday? Love to Enid.

　　　　　　　　　Yours Godfrey.

The small man

So it is obvious that if you are a bit careless, a doctor can give you a very hard time, in relation to, say, an insurance man or an undertaker. I mean, if you upset the insurance man, the worst he can do is flog you a dodgy premium and drop his bike on your geraniums; and a peevish undertaker can't do much except perhaps send you off with your coat on back to front, or your shoes on the wrong feet, wearing a funny hat which, compared with the machinations of an incensed medic, is all a bit junior league, if you see what I mean.

Another good reason for buttering up the National Health mob is because my wife is a hypochondriac of some eminence in these parts. She gets to inaugurate new waiting rooms, *and* she is in charge of the fish tank at Wimbledon General, *and* she's got her own chair at the chemist's dispensary in the High Street. She is frightened that the goodwill she has built up over the years – four hundred and eighty-six prescriptions in 1975, a British and Commonwealth record – will be negated if I keep knocking the sawbones – and let's face it, this lot of doctors we've got now, whatever their shortcomings, are a big improvement on their forebears who, as I remember, based their bedside manner on the philosophies of such members of the profession as Doctors Fu Manchu, Goebels, Crippen, Burke and Hare. In fact I recall that when I was a child there were definite laid down rules when sending for the doctor.

(A)   The patient must promise faithfully not to do anything stupid in the immediate future, like making a sudden recovery, or dying, so that he wastes the doctor's valuable time.

(B)   Everything in the house must be scrubbed, and if you can't scrub it, hide it.

(C)   The patient must be so washed that anything happening to him from then on can only come as a merciful release.

(D)   The patient must be warned against attempting to engage the doctor in frivolous conversation such as,

"*The worst thing that a stroppy undertaker can do is something like sending you off with your coat on back to front and wearing a funny hat.*"

"Good morning", "Am I going to get well again?" or "You're sitting on my arm."

(E)   The lady of the house must put on her best dress and practise smiling and opening the front door, then nipping smoothly out of the way so that she doesn't get trampled as he gallops past on his way up the stairs.

When he comes down again, she must accept the prescription for chalky water with humility and reverence as if she were receiving the last of the Dead Sea Scrolls.

Outbursts such as, "God bless you, sir, you're an angel sent from heaven above!" must be avoided, bearing in mind that he does have the power to get the poor old cow certified. Of course we've made a lot of progress since then, but I still think that British medicine has a lot to learn from the Americans. D'you remember the great days of Ben Casey and Doctor Kildare? Be honest, when did you last see a doctor take a good clout on the nut with a bedpan from a disgruntled sufferer?

And did good ol' Doctor Kildare hit him back? Of course not, he just got to his feet and said, "Thank heavens, I think the crisis has passed. A merry Christmas everybody!"

12

The small man

and keeping fit

> *My grandfather was fantastic –*
> *when he was a hundred he had*
> *all his own teeth, and*
> *so much hair that he actually died of dandruff.*

The small man

It is not generally realised that the maintainance of a maximum degree of physical fitness is even more important to the Small Man than it is to the Large Man. This is because, according to my information, it takes approximately a million billion germs to knock off a Large Man, but only half a dozen determined bacilli can wreak havoc with the average Small Man's more finely tuned, and more sensitive little bits and pieces.

Statistics show that if a Small Man and a Large Man are attacked by a certain virus at the same time, the Large Man will be sitting up drinking his Lucozade and reading his Beano, at the same time as the Small Man's relations are sitting around drinking his sherry and reading his will.

So, it is with a view to minimising this drain on the nation's most valuable citizens that I have compiled the following little guide to longevity:–

However, before launching yourself into the "Keep Fit Kick" as it is known to the medical profession, you should go and see your local G.P., because he might decide that you are not in good enough condition to start becoming healthy or that you must make the transition very gradually, starting by thinking kind thoughts and watching Match of the Day. He might even prescribe a course of tablets to make it all a bit easier for you. As a matter of fact, while we are being perfectly frank with each other, I must admit that I still take a few pills myself, just to sort of get the day started. I take a couple of red ones to get me to the bathroom, and a green one to make it worthwhile when I get there, and a white one to offset the side effects of the green one. And then it's just the little blue one to get me across the road without getting knocked over and a couple of black ones so that if I do get knocked down I'm going to enjoy it.

Actually a friend of mine, who is on the same treatment, happens to be a bit colour blind and he does have some very unusual mornings sometimes.

There are of course many and varied opinions as to what is and what is not good for you. During my researches into this subject, I have found some people who swore by jumping out of bed and taking deep breaths in front of an open window; some who jumped out of bed and took deep breaths in front of a closed window, and others who thought it best to breathe normally and not go anywhere near a window.

Even expert opinion is not infallible. For instance, early morning jogging, which was at first thought to be the ideal way of forcing oxygen into the lungs and bloodstream or wherever it goes to, is now shown to be capable of decimating the population faster than any known microbes, however early the latter get up in the morning.

In a random sample of a hundred early morning joggers in Central Park, New York, it was found that in one week thirty-five of them had been flattened by early morning motorists driving home from a party. Twenty-eight were mugged by early morning muggers; it is not clear whether these had been to a party or had got up early for the purpose. Three had sprained an ankle and got pneumonia waiting for a taxi, two were attacked by stray dogs, and one was shot by a policeman.

Whereas, of an equally random sample of citizens still in bed, only three fatalities were reported: two from natural

"*I take two yellow pills to give me the nerve to cross the road without getting run over, and a couple of black ones so that if I do get run over I'm going to enjoy it.*"

causes and one because he was in the wrong bed.

By the same token, the swinging of Indian Clubs, or Indian Club-Swinging, which was at one time thought to be a healthy method of toning up the muscles, has gone out of favour since it was noticed that many Indian Club-Swingers were found to become morose, unsociable and liable to fits of depression, caused by hitting themselves on the head during the more advanced routines.

The Victorians were probably the most enthusiastic Indian Club-Swingers, and one has only to look at any group photograph taken at the time to perceive obvious cases of advanced melancholia. The expression on the features of any statue of the late Queen Victoria is indeed proof enough that she must have been one of the most inefficient Club-Swingers of her day.

So, bearing in mind the pitfalls to be avoided, why not start with a couple of the old standard exercises such as, "Feet together – mouth shut – arms upwards stretch," which is not only good for the muscles but will get you full marks if you are ever in a bank holdup.

"Feet astride, touch your toes," is also a goody, but not altogether recommended for us Small Men, because we are so much nearer our toes than most people, and purposely touching them can become a bit demoralising if we're not careful. So much for exercises!

Of course no chapter on this subject would be complete without the most important piece of advice which is, *to avoid things that are bad for you.* "But," says you, "how am I to know what is bad for me?"

Well let's take things one at a time, starting with food. All food and drink is bad for you. That is to say all modern food and drink, and leading dieticians at Heidelberg University have proved beyond a shadow of doubt that if the Egyptians had had access to Keg Bitter, Egg and Chips, Takeaway Chinese or Colonel Sanders in 600 B.C., they would never have built the Pyramids. The fact that they fell down on the doors and windows, and therefore never found a buyer, is no reflection on the efficiency of the workers, but it is said to be due to a mixup with paperwork at the office.

The point is that if you can get down to a little maize pulp and mare's milk three times a day, your work output will increase and you will probably live to be a hundred; although naturally there will be times when you will wonder why you are living to be a hundred.

Smoking is bad for you. And as soon as you stop smoking you not only feel much fitter but you will notice that your senses are sharpened so that you become aware of things that escaped your notice before. Things like the chap across the road knocking out his pipe, and you will realise for the first time that his noise is a deliberate intrusion on your privacy and little does he realise that, because you are so fit, you will kill him if he keeps it up. You will also notice that everybody on television, except the newsreaders and Valerie Singleton, are smoking their heads off. And you suspect that the teams in Match of the Day go off and have a quick drag at half time. So that if you are to succeed in becoming a nonsmoker, you will have to become a selective viewer, and incidentally a selective reader as well, because in 98 per cent of all known library books someone, be it the herione, hero, detective or innocent bystander, will light one up and in some chapters they may all be at it at the same time on the very same page, and you will have to be a tower of strength not to join in.

Of course there is a certain amount of recommended reading such as, *What Katy did at School* and *What Katy did Next* by Susan Collidge. *Rattray's Pure Criticism of Common Logic,* and *Soil Erosion – its Cause and Effects* by Weller and Jackson, which might get you through the sticky period. But alas, there will always be weaklings who will fall by the wayside, and I well remember that evening when I threw down my *What Katy did at School* and addressed my wife as follows:–

"I think I'll take the dog for a walk."

"We haven't got a dog, he died last Christmas."

"He wouldn't have done if you'd looked after him!"

"He was twenty-six."

"Where's the cat, is he dead as well?"

"He's gone out."

"Well when he comes in, tell him that I've gone down to the King's Arms!!"

And even before I had taken my coat from the hallstand our children ran to clutch her skirts.

"Mummy, Mummy!" they piped. "Where is Daddy going?"

She lay her slightly careworn hands on their little heads, "I think that Daddy is forgetting his fine resolutions," she said. "And ere this night is out, he will be just as we have always known him, in short, a slob."

"Hurrah! Hurrah!" they cried. "Can we watch the telly?"

13

The small man

and holidays

> *My wife found some money in the bottom of the wardrobe which is rather a pity because I was saving it up for a surprise holiday for two in Majorca, and half of it belonged to the au pair.*

The small man

Actually holidays, like so many other things, are not all that different for the Small Man as for anybody else. To paraphrase the late William Shakespeare; if the rain falls on us do we not get wet?*** And if we go to the Barbeque and drink the Sangria do we not dance on the table and throw up in the coach?

The one thing the very Small Man on holiday must avoid is getting too involved with other people's children, because they are inclined to get a bit bossy and start sending you for things, so naturally you have to assert your dignity, which leads to childish reprisals like jumping on your castle or sticking your lolly in the sand. However, one of the marvellous things about living in these times is the variety of holiday outlets available to the average person, ranging from, "Send the Old Folks up the Orinoco", to a "Youth and Beauty Tour of Soho". Both of which, by the way, carry the government health warning. So let us consider some different types of holidays one at a time.

Boating. It is a fact that every year round about April, thousands of people start considering the river, some as the final answer to the yearly tax demand, and others as a good idea for a holiday.

And it is my personal experience that half a dozen friends

***If you leave us in the sun too long do we not fry?

can have a fairly enjoyable fortnight, "Cruising down the river in the Good Old Summer Time", as the song goes, for not much more than the price of a small row of houses.

A worthwhile tip when taking over a boat is to make sure to elect a captain. This is to ensure that there is someone to take the responsibility for difficult decisions such as, "*Shall we make fast for the night,*" or "*go astern,*" or "*hit the lock gates?*" "*Is old Soandso merely sleeping off the effects of the cider or shall we bury him at sea?*" "*If we throw a lifebelt in the river for Whatsisname who is going to pay supposing we lose it?*"

Driving a river cruiser is a fairly simple process. If you push the gear lever forward you might go forwards and if you push it backward you might go backwards. There are however no brakes so that if, as a beginner, you get the impression that all is not well and that disaster may be looming, it is best to brace yourself firmly against the nearest solid object and, covering the face with the hands, say, "Oh my God!"

Actually, for people who do suffer from this weakness for bouncing about on water, a cruise on an ocean liner is a preferable way of doing it, if only for the fact that if it does happen to sink you don't have the embarrassment of explaining what happened to the man it belongs to.

Camping. And of course the success of a camping holiday relies on so many factors, one of the most important being where you set up your tent. And to this end I asked a few people of my acquaintance where they would most like to put up a tent and the first one said, "In the penthouse at the Dorchester." And the next one replied, "What's a tent?" So I didn't ask any more of them.

To be honest, my only experience of camping was long ago when I was a Boy Scout. Members of the old Peewee Patrol where are you now? Don't call me and I won't call you. Dib! Dib! Dib!

Those were the days. Up early in the morning, a quick wash in a bucket of typhoid, then, "Come and get it!" And

The small man

off we'd go to the cooktent for our gastro-enteritis, after which we would form up into our Woodcraft Patrols, and, carrying our own dead, track into the woods to write down the names of as many stinging nettles as we could find. While back at base the Scoutmaster and Akela were left to spend the morning drinking tea and explaining their personal hangups to each other. I don't know if I can remember anymore useful tips which could be of help to the would-be camper.

I do recall something about tightening the guy ropes when it's raining, but I can't remember for certain whether you do tighten them or you don't tighten them. It might be as well to check this one before using one. I do know, however, that if someone breaks a leg you should tie it to the other leg. A useful tip which will raise a few eyebrows among those present, especially the chap with the broken leg.

So much for camping!

Holiday Camps. I recall that when I was discussing this chapter with my publisher I remarked that Holiday Camps are ideal for people with children, to which he replied, "Of course they are, if you don't tell the children which one you've gone to."

That remark gives us an insight into why so many publishers' larvae grow up to be bitter and twisted people and become in some cases television producers.

So I won't say anymore on the subject, except to reiterate that Holiday Camps *are* ideal for people with children, and I personally think you *should* tell them which one you've gone to – provided it's far away enough for them not to be able to afford the fare (in memorium W. C. FIELDS).

Pony Trekking. Here is a holiday that is simply great for people who like ponies and trekking. But as Cliff Michelmore might say on his programme about holidays, "If you hate the thought of it, then it's not for you."

Thank you, Cliff, and keep up the good work.

African Safari. There are apparently two distinctly different kinds of safari holidays.

(A)   You go to Africa and observe majestic denizens of the jungle as they roam wild and free in the breathtaking beauty of their natural surroundings and you take their pictures.

(B)   You go to Africa and observe majestic denizens of the jungle as they roam wild and free in the breathtaking beauty of their natural surroundings and you shoot them.

Of course shooting them with a gun instead of a camera does involve more of an element of danger because while a great many of the said denizens have been photographed before and see no harm in it, most of them can be very churlish about being shot, especially by an amateur in a baseball cap. Which is why a good safari outfit will carry an extensive first aid kit and a stack of will forms.

Putting the fact that you'll probably get killed aside for a moment, you have got to admit that a genuine trophy on the living room wall is a great conversation piece.

"I say, why have you got a pig's head on the wall? I thought you were Jewish."

"Oh that, that's not a pig's head, it's a wild boar. Anyway, I'm not really orthodox."

"Why is it on your wall?"

"I shot him in Africa when I was on safari last year."

"Oh I see. Did I tell you I'm thinking of buying a new Simca?"

"I caught him with a perfect shoulder shot with a Magnum 20.40 at a thousand yards."

"My dentist has got a Simca and he swears by 'em."

"Actually our White Hunter said he'd never seen a shot like it, in all his twenty five-years in the bush."

"Never had a day's trouble since he bought it."

"Those tusks could rip a man ———"

"He said his brother could get me one practically whole-sale."

The small man

"Will you shut up about your bloody motorcar!?"

"Well, if that's your attitude, I'll say goodnight! And wait till I tell Rabbi Symons that you've got a pig's head in the living room!"

Seaside. So last but, as they say, not least is the traditional British boarding house seaside holiday.

And to be perfectly honest – and how often do you meet somebody both perfect and honest these days? So make the most of me because we are a dying breed. But as I was saying, to be perfectly honest I do happen to be something of an expert on the seaside boarding house.

"What!" I can hear you cry. "How can you be an expert on the seaside boarding house? You with your big motorcar with the wind down windows and revolving hubcaps, and your Fan Club so exclusive that nobody joined."

The answer is simple. For years in company with many fellow performers I worked every summer in small seaside theatres, living in digs and boarding houses. I was so poor that often on a Sunday morning I would wander the streets with a piece of bread hoping to dip it in somebody's egg.

So that the next time you go to a seaside show and you hear the comedian saying things like –

"We always know when it's roly poly pudding for dinner because the landlady's only wearing one stocking."

Or –

"I said, 'Your doggy must like me, Mrs. Stompweasel. He just never takes his eyes off me.'

" 'That's because you're eating off his plate.' "

Or –

"She said, 'If you stay here you'll have to make your own bed.'

"I said, 'That's all right.'

"She said, 'Good, here's a hammer and nails, the timber is in the shed.' "

Or –

"*On Sunday morning I used to wander around Herne Bay with my piece of bread, hoping to dip it in somebody's egg.*"

The small man

"I said to the landlady, 'I've just bought a lovely T Bone steak for my supper. If I give it to you, will you put it in a saucepan of cold water and boil it?'

"She said, 'Yes.'

"I said, 'I thought you would.' "

– you have it on good authority that sometimes he is not too far from the truth.

14

The small man

and writing a book

> *You may remember my grandfather's autobiography of his fighting in the Boer War entitled,*
> I busted my guts for General Smuts.

Bookwriting, or authorship as it is called by people who can't spell bookwriting, is undoubtedly one of the easiest ways there is of becoming rich, taking second place only to making a hit record or joining the Mafia. So, if you can't sing and your local branch is full up, this is indeed your lucky day.

"But," I hear you say, "I don't know anything about writing, it takes me two days to send a postcard from Bournemouth." This tells me two things, A. that you are a painstaking perfectionist, and B. that you, by virtue of your inexperience, are a rich untapped source of natural talent, needing only a little push in the right direction to become a famous author, the envy of your friends and acquaintances. No party will be complete without you, and beautiful women will throw themselves at your feet, which sounds a bit painful but you'll get to like it once you are used to it.

Now everybody knows the hardest thing about writing a book is getting it started. But believe me once you've got a few good characters in Chapter One, it practically writes itself. All you have to do is get them unmasked, married, or killed off on page four hundred and sixteen so that it all ends happy ever after and the reader doesn't stay awake at nights thinking of ways to get his money back.

So, to save you sitting around waiting to get started, thereby losing valuable time which could be put to better purpose like dining with the Rainier's on your yacht, please read on below where you will find the first chapter of your first full length mystery novel, complete with a corpse and plenty of suspects just waiting to be completed and sent off.

Then when you have finished, forward the completed manuscript to the publishers of this book, enclosing your name and address and five hundred pounds in used notes to defray expenses such as printing, publishing, corruption etc, and the best of luck.

"*MURDER AT THE GRANGE*"

(This is a lovely title because it not only tells you what happened but where the action took place.)

"Well, this is a bit of a rum do, I must say," muttered Police Sergeant Dokes. "In all my years with the Northshire Force I can't say I've ever come across the likes of this before."

He turned from the body of Sir Jasper Aldwych, wealthy financier and part time blues pianist, which was slumped across the great mahogany desk, the jewelled hilt of the dagger in his back reflecting the dancing flames of the big log fire in the open hearth.

The Sergeant crossed to where, on the far side of the oak-panelled study, the figure of a lovely young girl of some twenty summers sat motionless in the leather armchair.

"There, there, my dear," he said, his tone gruff but kindly, "I expect all this has come as a bit of a shock to you?"

Lady Agatha glanced across at the body of her father and nodded, her eyes moistened. "Oh, who could have perpertrated this dreadful deed?" she whispered.

"That, my dear, is just what I intend to find out," said Sergeant Dokes producing from his breast pocket a note book and pencil.

"You do realise I shall have to ask you some questions?"

"Yes, I suppose you will," she replied, dabbing her eyes

The small man

with a tiny handkerchief.

"Have you ever heard voices raised in anger coming from this room?"

She nodded, "Yes, I have."

"When?"

"All the time, you might say that this room is never without raised voices coming from it."

He turned to a fresh page of his notebook. "Do you ever recognise any of these voices?"

"Yes, I do, Sergeant, sometimes it's the cook, who my father accuses of trying to poison him, and why else would she want a sack of weedkiller in her bedroom?"

The policeman looked across at the lifeless cadaver. "It's a pity he wasn't poisoned," he said. "We could have wrapped this case up in no time at all, as you might say."

She nodded sympathetically and continued, "And sometimes it was the under footman, whom Daddy accused of being after my body. He is on a week's notice, and will be sadly missed."

The Sergeant stopped scribbling and looked up sharply. "I noticed the lad when I arrived here," he said. "I'd say he's got gypsy blood in his veins."

She smiled, "Well, if you've got gypsy blood, that's the best place to have it, I should think, it stops it getting on the furniture."

(A little bit of humour here – they like that – but don't overdo it.)

He tried to repress a smile. "I'll say that for you, Miss, you're a plucky 'un, and no mistake. Anyone else?"

"Yes, there's the butler, he is a well-known psycopath, but Daddy took him on because he suffers from amnesia and sometimes forgets to ask for his wages. And least but not last is my twin brother, a transvestite compulsive gambler who specialises in blackmail and dreams of a plan to kill everybody in the world and keep all the money for himself."

The Sergeant lit a cigarette, inhaled deeply, and looked at her thoughtfully for a few moments. "I don't suppose you'd get many of those to the pound?" he said at last.

Lady Agatha followed the direction of his eyes down the top of her dress and a blush diffused the pallor of her cheeks.

"No, I don't suppose you would," she murmured.

(Just a hint of sex here, which is all right if it's carefully worked into the context.)

"Now have you seen any furtive strangers hanging about the grounds lately?" he continued.

The girl's lovely face clouded. "It's funny that you should ask that, because you can never put a foot out of the door of late without coming into contact with a furtive stranger, mostly swarthy with staring eyes."

The Sergeant stopped writing and glanced up. "Now I think we are getting somewhere at last. They appear to be foreigners. Did your father have any enemies abroad?"

She was silent for a few moments, thinking. "Yes, he did have some enemies."

"How many?"

"Well it's hard to be specific, but I do know that nobody liked him in South East Asia, that's including the People's Republic of Outer Mongolia and Tashkent. And all of his friends in the Lower Congo Basin could be got into a phone-box, if they had one. It is also said that certain wandering tribes of the Kalahari are still using his name as an emetic in cases of emergency; and how the Japanese knew that Daddy was out fishing that day at Pearl Harbor, I shall never know."

Sergeant Dokes smiled slightly and nodded. "I think at last a pattern is beginning to emerge. Just one more question, did your father ever speak of suicide?"

She sighed deeply. "Poor Daddy, he seldom spoke of anything else."

NOW WRITE ON

(I personally think that when all these suspects have been eliminated we shall find that Sergeant Dokes did it because Sir Jasper once had a bit of a thing going with Dokes's young sister, who ended it all when he chucked her out and she jumped – fell – or was pushed off the top of a brothel in Buenos Aires.)

The small man

So finally dear reader, I hope that if you are a Small Man you have found something in the foregoing to inspire you to look the world straight in the kneecap and cry, "Small is Beautiful!" and "The Best Things in Life are Small!" And at the risk of being called a sentimental fool may I leave you with a little poem that my mother used to say to me when she tucked me up in my little cot every morning.

A POEM

Never look down on a Biggie,
It can't be so nice to be tall.
They keep hitting their heads,
They're too long for their beds.
When they're drunk
They've got further to fall.
So never look down on a Biggie,
Remember it might have been you.
Let us think for a sec
Of Toulouse and Lautrec,
To name not just one but a few.
Never look down on a Biggie,
Look up, that's all you can do.
And if Goering and Hitler
Had been a bit littler
We'd never have had World War Two.

(About here she always broke down and cried and with lines like that who can blame her.)

Remember Brothers, Walk Small!